TEN WALLS OF THE FUTURE

By Jesse E. Cleverson

ISBN – 9798215744758

TABLE OF CONTENTS

Introduction

Please be aware that blank pages are included in this book for personal use. These pages can be used for taking notes or writing down any important information you may want to refer back to. ENJOY READING.

INTRODUCTION

Welcome to **"Ten Walls of the Future"**, a comprehensive guide to the top 10 businesses that are poised to dominate the market in the coming years. In this book, we delve into a diverse range of industries, from health and education to graphics and humanities. We also explore the impact of emerging technologies on various businesses. Each chapter is dedicated to a specific business and delves into the current trends and future potential of that industry. Whether you're an entrepreneur looking for inspiration or a professional looking to stay ahead of the curve, "Ten Walls of the Future" is an essential guide to the business world of tomorrow.

CHAPTER 1
CONTENT MARKETING

Content marketing is a strategic marketing approach focused on creating and distributing valuable, relevant, and consistent content to attract and retain a clearly defined audience, and ultimately, to drive profitable customer action.

Content marketing aims to provide valuable information to consumers and build trust with them. This can be in the form of blog posts, videos, social media posts, emails, or other forms of content.

Some examples of content marketing include:

Blog posts on a company's website about topics related to their industry

Videos on YouTube demonstrating how to use a company's products

Social media posts featuring customer testimonials or success stories

Emails to a company's email list with valuable tips or resources related to the company's products or services

Ebooks or whitepapers offered for download in exchange for an email address

A brief on why content marketing is a business of the future.

Content marketing is a business of the future for several reasons.

First and foremost, the internet and social media have completely transformed the way businesses reach and interact with customers. In the past, businesses relied on traditional forms of marketing such as television commercials, radio ads, and print advertisements to get their message out to the public. These methods were often expensive and not very targeted, making it difficult to reach the right audience.

On the other hand, content marketing allows businesses to directly target their audience through online channels. By creating valuable and relevant content, businesses can attract and retain a clearly defined audience and ultimately drive profitable customer action. This can be achieved through a variety of content types such as blog posts, videos, social media posts, and more.

Furthermore, the rise of mobile devices and the ubiquity of the internet have made it easier than ever for consumers to access information and make purchasing decisions. According to a study by Google, over half of all internet searches are now conducted on a mobile device. This means that businesses need to have a strong online presence in order to reach their target audience. Content marketing is an effective way for businesses to establish themselves as thought leaders in their industry and attract potential customers through search engines and social media.

Another reason why content marketing is a business of the future is because it allows for more personalized and authentic interactions with customers. In the past, businesses often used generic marketing messages to reach a mass audience. However, today's consumers are savvier and are seeking out personalized and authentic experiences. By creating and distributing valuable, relevant, and consistent content, businesses can build trust with their audience and create a more personalized experience.

Finally, content marketing is a cost-effective way for businesses to reach and engage with their audience. Traditional forms of marketing can be expensive and may not always produce the desired results. On the other hand, content marketing allows businesses to reach a targeted audience at a fraction of the cost of traditional marketing methods. Additionally, the ROI of content marketing can be measured more accurately through metrics such as website traffic, leads generated, and conversions.

In conclusion, content marketing is a business of the future because it allows businesses to reach and engage with their target audience in a cost-effective and personalized way. With the rise of the internet and mobile devices, having a strong online presence is essential for businesses to succeed in today's digital age. By creating and distributing valuable, relevant, and consistent content, businesses can attract and retain a clearly defined audience and ultimately drive profitable customer action.

How can people prepare for this?

As the use of content marketing continues to grow and evolve, it's important for professionals to stay up-to-date and prepared for the future. Here are a few ways that people can prepare for the future of content marketing as professionals:

Stay up-to-date with industry trends and best practices: The field of content marketing is constantly changing, so it's important to stay informed about the latest trends and best practices. This can be achieved through reading industry blogs, attending conferences and workshops, and networking with other professionals.

Develop a diverse set of skills: In order to be successful in content marketing, it's important to have a diverse set of skills. This may include writing, design, video production, and social media management, among others. Consider taking courses or earning certifications to expand your skillset and stay competitive in the industry.

Learn about SEO: Search engine optimization (SEO) is a crucial aspect of content marketing. By understanding how to optimize your content for search engines, you can increase its visibility and drive more traffic to your website.

Stay agile and adaptable: The field of content marketing is constantly changing, so it's important to stay agile and adaptable. This means being open to new ideas, technologies, and strategies, and being willing to pivot when necessary.

Experiment with new platforms and technologies: In order to stay ahead of the curve, it's important to be willing to experiment with new platforms and technologies. This could include trying out new social media platforms, exploring new types of content, or incorporating emerging technologies such as virtual reality or artificial intelligence into your content marketing strategy.

By staying up-to-date, developing a diverse set of skills, learning about SEO, staying agile and adaptable, and experimenting with new platforms and technologies, professionals can prepare for the future of content marketing and make the most out of it.

Five top programs that can help you be an expert in that field

Here are five programs that can be studied to make a person an expert in content marketing for the future:

Master's degree in Marketing: A master's degree in marketing can provide a comprehensive education in the principles and practices of marketing, including content marketing. Many programs offer coursework in areas such as digital marketing, social media marketing, and content strategy.

Certificate program in Content Marketing: Certificate programs in content marketing are often focused specifically on the skills and strategies needed to create and distribute effective content. These programs may cover topics such as content planning, production, distribution, and measurement.

Online courses in Content Marketing: Online courses in content marketing are a flexible and convenient option for those looking to gain expertise in the field. Many courses offer hands-on learning opportunities and allow students to work at their own pace.

Internship or apprenticeship: An internship or apprenticeship in content marketing can provide practical experience and allow individuals to learn from experienced professionals. These programs often provide hands-on training and the opportunity to work on real-world projects.

Professional certifications: Professional certifications, such as the Certified Content Marketer (CCM) credential offered by the Content Marketing Institute, can demonstrate expertise in the field and can be beneficial for career advancement. These programs often require the completion of coursework and the passing of an exam.

Overall, there are many different programs and resources available for those looking to become experts in content marketing for the future. The best option will depend on an individual's goals, interests, and schedule.

Advice for up and coming young people

Here are a few pieces of advice for upcoming young people looking to succeed in the field of content marketing:

Learn as much as you can: The field of content marketing is constantly evolving, so it's important to stay up-to-date on the latest trends and best practices. Consider taking courses or earning certifications to expand your knowledge and skills.

Build a strong online presence: Having a strong online presence is essential for success in the field of content marketing. This includes maintaining a professional website and social media accounts, and regularly creating and sharing high-quality content.

Network and seek out opportunities: Networking and seeking out opportunities can help you build relationships and gain experience in the field. Consider attending conferences, joining industry groups, and interning or apprenticing with a content marketing professional.

Be adaptable and open to change: The field of content marketing is always changing, so it's important to be adaptable and open to new ideas and approaches. Be willing to try new things and pivot when necessary.

Keep learning and growing: Finally, it's important to continue learning and growing throughout your career. This can include staying up-to-date on industry trends, learning new skills, and seeking out new opportunities for professional development.

Potential earnings as a professional in the field

According to data from the Bureau of Labor Statistics, the median annual wage for public relations specialists, which includes content marketers, was $61,150 in May 2020. However, wages can range from less than $33,820 for the bottom 10 percent to more than $124,520 for the top 10 percent.

Earnings for content marketing professionals may also vary based on job role. For example, a content marketing manager or director may earn a higher salary than a content marketing specialist or coordinator.

Ultimately, potential earnings for a professional in the field of content marketing in the future will depend on a variety of factors and can vary widely. It's important to consider these factors and do your own research when considering earning potential in the field.

Some successful figures in the niche

One of the most successful people in the field of content marketing is Ann Handley. Ann is the Chief Content Officer of MarketingProfs and the author of the best-selling book, "Everybody Writes: Your Go-To Guide to Creating Ridiculously Good Content."

Ann has had a long and successful career in content marketing, beginning as a writer and editor at The Boston Globe and later joining MarketingProfs in 2001. Since then, she has built MarketingProfs into one of the leading online resources for marketing professionals, with a focus on creating high-quality, valuable content.

Ann's work has been recognized by numerous industry awards and accolades, including being named a Top 10 Content Marketer by The Script, one of Forbes' Top 50 Social Media Power Influencers, and one of LinkedIn's Top Voices in Marketing and Social Media.

In addition to her work at MarketingProfs, Ann is also a popular speaker and trainer, teaching workshops and keynote presentations around the world on the topics of content marketing, writing, and social media.

CHAPTER 2
VIRTUAL EDUCATION/ONLINE TRAINING

Virtual education, also known as online education or e-learning, is a form of education that is delivered via the internet. Online training is a type of virtual education that is focused on providing specific skills or knowledge to individuals or organizations.

Virtual education and online training can take many forms, including:

Online courses: These are structured educational programs that are typically delivered through a learning management system (LMS) and may include video lectures, readings, quizzes, and assignments.

Webinars: These are live or recorded online presentations that are typically focused on a specific topic or skill.

Virtual workshops or seminars: These are interactive sessions that may include live lectures, discussions, and hands-on activities.

Virtual coaching or tutoring: These are one-on-one or small group sessions with a coach or tutor who provides guidance and support to learners.

Virtual education and online training can be a convenient and flexible way for individuals and organizations to learn new skills or gain knowledge in a particular area. They can be particularly useful for those who are unable to attend in-person training due to location or other constraints.

A brief on why virtual education/online training is a business of the future.

Virtual education and online training are businesses of the future for several reasons.

First and foremost, the internet and advances in technology have made it easier than ever for individuals and organizations to access educational content online. With the rise of mobile devices and the ubiquity of the internet, it's now possible for people to learn new skills or gain knowledge from anywhere in the world.

Another reason why virtual education and online training are businesses of the future is because they offer a convenient and flexible way for people to learn. With traditional in-person education, individuals and organizations may need to take time off work or travel long distances to attend classes. Virtual education and online training allow learners to access content on their own schedule, making it easier to fit learning into their busy lives.

In addition, virtual education and online training can be more cost-effective than traditional in-person education. While there may be upfront costs to develop and deliver online content, the overall costs of virtual education and online training are often lower than those of traditional in-person education due to the lack of physical infrastructure and other overhead expenses.

Finally, virtual education and online training can reach a wider audience than traditional in-person education. By delivering content online, educators can reach learners around the world, potentially increasing their reach and impact.

Overall, virtual education and online training are businesses of the future due to the convenience, flexibility, cost-effectiveness, and reach that they offer. As technology continues to evolve, it's likely that virtual education and online training will become an increasingly important part of the education landscape.

How can people prepare for this?

Here are a few ways that people can prepare for a career in the business of virtual education and online training:

Gain expertise in a subject area: To be successful in the business of virtual education and online training, it's important to have a deep understanding of the subject matter that you will be teaching. Consider earning a degree or certification in your area of expertise or gaining practical experience through work or internships.

Learn about instructional design: Instructional design is the process of creating educational content in a way that is effective and engaging for learners. To be successful in the business of virtual education and online training, it's important to have a strong understanding of instructional design principles and best practices.

Develop your teaching skills: Teaching online requires a different set of skills than teaching in-person. Consider taking courses or workshops to develop your skills in areas such as online facilitation, course design, and assessment.

Stay up-to-date with technology: The field of virtual education and online training is constantly evolving, so it's important to stay up-to-date with the latest technologies and platforms. This may include learning about different learning management systems, video conferencing tools, and other technologies that are commonly used in online education.

Network and seek out opportunities: Networking and seeking out opportunities can help you build relationships and gain experience in the field. Consider joining professional organizations, attending conferences, and connecting with others in the industry to learn about job opportunities and stay up-to-date on the latest trends.

By gaining expertise in a subject area, learning about instructional design, developing your teaching skills, staying up-to-date with technology, and networking and seeking out opportunities, you can prepare for a career in the business of virtual education and online training.

Five top programs that can help you be an expert in that field

Here are five programs that can help you become an expert in the field of virtual education and online training:

Master's degree in Education with a focus on online learning: A master's degree in education with a focus on online learning can provide a comprehensive education in the principles and practices of virtual education and online training. Many programs offer coursework in areas such as instructional design, course development, and online facilitation.

Certificate program in Online Teaching: Certificate programs in online teaching are focused specifically on the skills and strategies needed to teach effectively online. These programs may cover topics such as course design, online facilitation, and assessment.

Online courses in Instructional Design: Online courses in instructional design can provide a deep understanding of the principles and practices of creating effective educational content. These courses may cover topics such as learning theories, course development, and assessment.

Internship or apprenticeship: An internship or apprenticeship in virtual education or online training can provide practical experience and allow individuals to learn from experienced professionals. These programs often provide hands-on training and the opportunity to work on real-world projects.

Professional certifications: Professional certifications, such as the Certified Online Instructor (COI) credential offered by the Online Learning Consortium, can demonstrate expertise in the field and can be beneficial for career advancement. These programs often require the completion of coursework and the passing of an exam.

Overall, there are many different programs and resources available for those looking to become experts in the field of virtual education and online training. The best option will depend on an individual's goals, interests, and schedule.

Advice for up and coming young people

Here are a few pieces of advice for upcoming young people looking to succeed in the field of virtual education and online training:

Gain expertise in a subject area: To be successful in virtual education and online training, it's important to have a deep understanding of the subject matter that you will be teaching. Consider earning a degree or certification in your area of expertise or gaining practical experience through work or internships.

Learn about instructional design: Instructional design is a crucial aspect of virtual education and online training. By understanding how to create effective and engaging educational content, you can improve the learning experience for your students.

Develop your teaching skills: Teaching online requires a different set of skills than teaching in-person. Consider taking courses or workshops to develop your skills in areas such as online facilitation, course design, and assessment.

Stay up-to-date with technology: The field of virtual education and online training is constantly evolving, so it's important to stay up-to-date with the latest technologies and platforms. This may include learning about different learning management systems, video conferencing tools, and other technologies that are commonly used in online education.

Network and seek out opportunities: Networking and seeking out opportunities can help you build relationships and gain experience in the field. Consider joining professional organizations, attending conferences, and connecting with others in the industry to learn about job opportunities and stay up-to-date on the latest trends.

By following these pieces of advice, upcoming young people can set themselves up for success in the field of virtual education and online training.

Potential earnings as a professional in the field

Earnings can vary based on factors such as experience, education, location, and job role.

According to data from the Bureau of Labor Statistics, the median annual wage for postsecondary teachers, which includes online instructors, was $79,540 in May 2020. However, wages can range from less than $41,880 for the bottom 10 percent to more than $170,910 for the top 10 percent.

Earnings for professionals in the field of virtual education and online training may also vary based on job role. For example, an instructional designer or course developer may earn a higher salary than an online instructor or teaching assistant.

Ultimately, potential earnings for a professional in the field of virtual education and online training in the future will depend on a variety of factors and can vary widely. It's important to consider these factors and do your own research when considering earning potential in the field.

Some successful figures in the niche

One of the most successful people in the field of virtual education and online training is Sal Khan. Sal is the founder and CEO of Khan Academy, a non-profit organization that provides free online educational content to learners around the world.

Sal started Khan Academy in 2004 as a way to tutor his younger cousin remotely. As he recorded more and more lessons, he began to receive requests from other students and teachers to access his content. In 2006, he launched Khan Academy as a full-fledged online education platform.

Since then, Khan Academy has grown into a global phenomenon, with millions of users accessing its content each month. In addition to providing free educational content, Khan Academy has also developed partnerships with schools and districts around the world to integrate its content into classrooms and support student learning.

Sal's work has been recognized with numerous awards and accolades, including being named one of Time's 100 Most Influential People and receiving a Kennedy Center Honor. In addition to his work at Khan Academy, Sal is also a popular speaker and author, sharing his insights on education and technology with audiences around the world.

Overall, Sal Khan is a shining example of success in the field of virtual education and online training. Through his dedication to providing high-quality, accessible educational content, he has built a successful organization and has helped to transform the way that people learn around the world.

CHAPTER 3
3D PRINTING

3D printing, also known as additive manufacturing, is a process of creating a three-dimensional object by building it up layer by layer using a machine. 3D printing technology has the potential to revolutionize the way that products are designed, developed, and manufactured.

There are many different 3D printing technologies, each with its own specific capabilities and limitations. Here are a few examples of 3D printing technologies:

Fused Deposition Modeling (FDM): This is the most common type of 3D printing technology. It works by heating and extruding a plastic or composite material through a nozzle, building up the object layer by layer.

Stereolithography (SLA): This technology uses a laser to cure layers of a photopolymer resin, building up the object layer by layer. SLA is known for producing high-quality, accurate parts.

Selective Laser Sintering (SLS): This technology uses a laser to sinter powdered materials, such as metals or plastics, building up the object layer by layer. SLS is often used to produce complex, high-strength parts.

Digital Light Processing (DLP): This technology uses a digital projector to cure layers of a photopolymer resin, building up the object layer by layer. DLP is known for producing high-resolution parts with fine details.

These are just a few examples of the many different 3D printing technologies that are available. As the field of 3D printing continues to evolve, new technologies and materials are being developed that have the potential to revolutionize the way that products are made.

A brief on why 3D printing is a business of the future.
3D printing is a business of the future for several reasons.

First and foremost, 3D printing has the potential to revolutionize the way that products are designed, developed, and manufactured. By enabling the production of complex, customized parts and products on-demand, 3D printing could significantly reduce the need for traditional manufacturing processes, such as injection molding and machining.

Another reason why 3D printing is a business of the future is because it has the potential to reduce waste and increase sustainability. Traditional manufacturing processes often produce a large amount of waste, whereas 3D printing produces minimal waste and can even use recycled materials as feedstock.

In addition, 3D printing has the potential to democratize manufacturing, allowing individuals and small businesses to produce their own products without the need for expensive tools and equipment. This could lead to the proliferation of small-scale manufacturing and the creation of new business opportunities.

Finally, 3D printing is a rapidly growing market, with the global 3D printing market size expected to reach $42.3 billion by 2027, according to data from Markets and Markets. This growth is being driven by increasing demand for 3D printing in a variety of industries, including healthcare, aerospace, and automotive.

Overall, 3D printing is a business of the future due to its potential to revolutionize the way that products are made, reduce waste and increase sustainability, democratize manufacturing, and tap into a rapidly growing market.

How can people prepare for this?

Here are a few ways that people can prepare for a career in the business of 3D printing:

Gain expertise in 3D printing technology: To be successful in the business of 3D printing, it's important to have a deep understanding of the different 3D printing technologies and how they work. Consider taking courses or earning a degree in a field such as mechanical engineering or manufacturing to gain expertise in 3D printing technology.

Learn about design and modeling software: 3D printing relies on computer-aided design (CAD) software to create digital models of the objects that will be printed. Familiarity with

CAD software, such as AutoCAD or SolidWorks, can be beneficial for a career in 3D printing.

Develop your skills in product design and development: 3D printing allows for the creation of customized and complex parts and products. Developing your skills in product design and development can help you create innovative and successful products using 3D printing technology.

Stay up-to-date with industry trends: The field of 3D printing is constantly evolving, so it's important to stay up-to-date with the latest trends and technologies. Consider joining professional organizations, attending conferences, and reading industry news to stay informed about developments in the field.

Network and seek out opportunities: Networking and seeking out opportunities can help you build relationships and gain experience in the field. Consider joining professional organizations, attending conferences, and connecting with others in the industry to learn about job opportunities and stay up-to-date on the latest trends.

By gaining expertise in 3D printing technology, learning about design and modeling software, developing your skills in product design and development, staying up-to-date with industry trends, and networking and seeking out opportunities, you can prepare for a career in the business of 3D printing and make the most of it.

Five top programs that can help you be an expert in that field

Here are five programs that can help you become an expert in the field of 3D printing:

Bachelor's degree in Mechanical Engineering: A bachelor's degree in mechanical engineering can provide a strong foundation in the principles and practices of 3D printing and other manufacturing technologies. Coursework may include topics such as computer-aided design (CAD), prototyping, and materials science.

Master's degree in Manufacturing: A master's degree in manufacturing can provide advanced training in the principles and practices of 3D printing and other manufacturing technologies. Coursework may include topics such as advanced CAD, prototyping, and materials science.

Certificate program in 3D Printing: Certificate programs in 3D printing are focused specifically on the principles and practices of 3D printing technology. These programs may cover topics such as 3D printing technologies, design and modeling software, and applications of 3D printing in various industries.

Online courses in 3D Printing: Online courses in 3D printing can provide a comprehensive overview of the principles and practices of 3D printing technology. These courses may cover topics such as 3D printing technologies, design and modeling software, and applications of 3D printing in various industries.

Internship or apprenticeship: An internship or apprenticeship in a 3D printing company or organization can provide practical experience and allow individuals to learn from experienced professionals. These programs often provide hands-on training and the opportunity to work on real-world projects.

Overall, there are many different programs and resources available for those looking to become experts in the field of 3D printing. The best option will depend on an individual's goals, interests, and schedule.

Advice for up and coming young people

Here are a few pieces of advice for upcoming young people looking to succeed in the field of 3D printing or any other field:

Set goals and work towards them: Having clear goals can help you stay motivated and focused on your long-term aspirations. Consider setting both short-term and long-term goals for yourself and developing a plan to achieve them.

Learn from your mistakes: Everyone makes mistakes, but it's important to learn from them and use them as opportunities for growth. When you make a mistake, try to understand what went wrong and how you can avoid making the same mistake in the future.

Be open to learning new things: The field of 3D printing and other fields are constantly evolving, so it's important to be open to learning new things and staying up-to-date with the latest trends and technologies. Consider taking courses or seeking out learning opportunities to continue developing your skills and knowledge.

Seek out mentors: Having a mentor can be a valuable resource for guidance and support. Consider seeking out mentors who are experienced professionals in the field and can provide guidance and support as you develop your career.

Network and build relationships: Building relationships and networking can help you learn about job opportunities and stay connected to the industry. Consider joining professional organizations, attending conferences, and connecting with others in the industry to build your network and expand your opportunities.

By setting goals, learning from your mistakes, being open to learning new things, seeking out mentors, and networking and building relationships, you can develop a positive attitude and set yourself up for success in the field of 3D printing and beyond.

Potential earnings as a professional in the field

Earnings can vary based on factors such as experience, education, location, and job role.

According to data from the Bureau of Labor Statistics, the median annual wage for mechanical engineers, which includes those working in 3D printing, was $88,430 in May 2020. However, wages can range from less than $56,910 for the bottom 10 percent to more than $144,520 for the top 10 percent.

Earnings for professionals in the field of 3D printing may also vary based on job role. For example, a 3D printing engineer or designer may earn a higher salary than a 3D printing technician or operator.

Ultimately, potential earnings for a professional in the field of 3D printing in the future will depend on a variety of factors and can vary widely. It's important to consider these factors and do your own research when considering earning potential in the field.

Some successful figures in that niche

One of the most successful people in the field of 3D printing is Scott Crump, the co-founder and CEO of Stratasys, a leading manufacturer of 3D printing systems.

Scott co-founded Stratasys in 1989 with his wife, Lisa Crump, and has played a key role in the company's growth and success. Under Scott's leadership, Stratasys has become a global leader in 3D printing, with a strong presence in a variety of industries including aerospace, automotive, and healthcare.

Scott has been recognized for his contributions to the field of 3D printing with numerous awards and accolades, including the Society of Manufacturing Engineers (SME) Outstanding Young Manufacturing Engineer Award and the Minnesota High Tech Association's Tekne Award for CEO of the Year.

Scott is also a strong advocate for the potential of 3D printing to revolutionize manufacturing and has spoken about the technology at conferences and events around the world.

Overall, Scott Crump is a shining example of success in the field of 3D printing. Through his dedication to innovation and leadership at Stratasys, he has helped to shape the future of manufacturing and has helped to make 3D printing a mainstream technology

CHAPTER 4
MENTAL HEALTH AND MARRIAGE COUNSELLING BUSINESS

Mental health counseling is a form of therapy that helps individuals address and manage their emotional, psychological, and behavioral well-being. Mental health counselors may work with clients on a variety of issues, including anxiety, depression, stress, substance abuse, and relationship problems.

Marriage counseling, also known as couples therapy, is a form of therapy that helps couples improve their relationship and address any issues or challenges they may be facing. Marriage counselors may work with couples on a variety of issues, including communication, conflict resolution, infidelity, and intimacy.

Here are a few examples of mental health and marriage counseling businesses:

Private practice: Many mental health counselors and marriage counselors work in private practice, where they see clients on an individual or couples basis. Private practices may offer a range of services, including individual therapy, couples therapy, group therapy, and online therapy.

Community mental health centers: Community mental health centers provide mental health and substance abuse services to underserved populations. Mental health counselors and marriage counselors may work at these centers to provide therapy and support to individuals and families.

Nonprofit organizations: Nonprofit organizations, such as churches or advocacy groups, may provide mental health and marriage counseling services to their communities. Counselors may work on a volunteer or paid basis to provide support to individuals and families in need.

Employee assistance programs: Many employers offer employee assistance programs (EAPs) to provide mental health and other support services to their employees. Mental health counselors and marriage counselors may work at these programs to provide therapy and support to employees.

Overall, mental health and marriage counseling businesses can take many forms, including private practices, community mental health centers, nonprofit organizations, and employee assistance programs.

A brief on why Mental Health and Marriage Counselling Business is a business of the future.

Mental health and marriage counseling businesses are a business of the future for several reasons.

First and foremost, there is a growing need for mental health and marriage counseling services. According to the World Health Organization, approximately 1 in 4 people will experience a mental health disorder at some point in their lives. Additionally, the demand for marriage counseling and other relationship support services is also increasing, as more and more couples seek help to improve their relationships and address challenges.

Another reason why mental health and marriage counseling businesses are a business of the future is because they have the potential to have a positive impact on individuals, families, and communities. By helping people manage their mental health and improve their relationships, these businesses can help to promote overall well-being and improve quality of life.

Finally, mental health and marriage counseling businesses are well-suited to the digital age, as many counseling services are now offered online or via teletherapy. This allows for increased accessibility and convenience for clients, which can help to increase demand for these services.

Overall, mental health and marriage counseling businesses are a business of the future due to the growing need for these services, their potential to have a positive impact, and their adaptability to the digital age.

How can people prepare for this?

Here are a few ways that people can prepare for a career in mental health and marriage counseling:

Earn a degree: Most mental health counselors and marriage counselors hold at least a bachelor's degree in a field such as psychology, social work, or counseling. A master's degree is often required to become a licensed mental health counselor or marriage and family therapist.

Gain experience: Many mental health counseling and marriage counseling programs include a practicum or internship component, which provides the opportunity to gain hands-on experience working with clients. Additionally, volunteering or working in related fields, such as social work or community mental health, can provide valuable experience and help build your resume.

Obtain certification or licensure: Mental health counselors and marriage counselors are typically required to be licensed or certified to practice in their state. The requirements for licensure or certification vary by state, but often include completing a degree program, passing an exam, and meeting certain experience requirements.

Stay up-to-date with industry trends: The field of mental health counseling and marriage counseling is constantly evolving, so it's important to stay up-to-date with the latest trends and best practices. Consider joining professional organizations, attending conferences, and reading industry news to stay informed about developments in the field.

Seek out mentors: Having a mentor can be a valuable resource for guidance and support. Consider seeking out mentors who are experienced professionals in the field and can provide guidance and support as you develop your career.

By earning a degree, gaining experience, obtaining certification or licensure, staying up-to-date with industry trends, and seeking out mentors, you can prepare for a career in mental health and marriage counseling and set yourself up for success.

Five top programs that can help you be an expert in that field

Here are five programs that can help you become an expert in the field of mental health and marriage counseling:

Bachelor's degree in Psychology, Social Work, or Counseling: A bachelor's degree in psychology, social work, or counseling can provide a strong foundation in the principles and practices of mental health and marriage counseling. Coursework may include topics such as human development, counseling techniques, and mental health disorders.

Master's degree in Counseling or Marriage and Family Therapy: A master's degree in counseling or marriage and family therapy can provide advanced training in the principles and practices of mental health and marriage counseling. Coursework may include topics such as counseling theories, assessment and diagnosis, and treatment planning.

Certificate program in Mental Health Counseling or Marriage and Family Therapy: Certificate programs in mental health counseling or marriage and family therapy are focused specifically on the principles and practices of these fields. These programs may cover topics such as counseling theories, assessment and diagnosis, and treatment planning.

Online courses in Mental Health Counseling or Marriage and Family Therapy: Online courses in mental health counseling or marriage and family therapy can provide a comprehensive overview of the principles and practices of these fields. These courses may cover topics such as counseling theories, assessment and diagnosis, and treatment planning.

Internship or apprenticeship: An internship or apprenticeship in a mental health counseling or marriage counseling practice or organization can provide practical experience and allow individuals to learn from experienced professionals. These programs often provide hands-on training and the opportunity to work on real-world projects.

Overall, there are many different programs and resources available for those looking to become experts in the field of mental health and marriage counseling. The best option will depend on an individual's goals, interests, and schedule.

Advice for up and coming young people

Here are a few pieces of advice for upcoming young people looking to succeed in the field of mental health and marriage counseling:

Believe in your ability to make a difference: Mental health and marriage counseling can be rewarding and fulfilling work, as you have the opportunity to make a positive impact on the lives of others. Believe in your ability to make a difference and let that belief motivate you to excel in your career.

Develop strong communication and interpersonal skills: Communication and interpersonal skills are essential for success in mental health and marriage counseling. Practice active listening, empathy, and assertiveness to build strong relationships with your clients and help them feel heard and understood.

Stay up-to-date with best practices and industry trends: The field of mental health and marriage counseling is constantly evolving, so it's important to stay up-to-date with the latest best practices and industry trends. Consider joining professional organizations, attending conferences, and reading industry news to stay informed about developments in the field.

Seek out mentors: Having a mentor can be a valuable resource for guidance and support. Consider seeking out mentors who are experienced professionals in the field and can provide guidance and support as you develop your career.

Take care of yourself: Mental health and marriage counseling can be emotionally demanding work, so it's important to take care of yourself and practice self-care. Set boundaries, make time for self-care activities, and seek support when needed to help you maintain a healthy work-life balance.

By developing strong communication and interpersonal skills, staying up-to-date with best practices and industry trends, seeking out mentors, and taking care of yourself, you can develop a positive attitude and set yourself up for success in the field of mental health and marriage counseling.

Potential earnings per year as a professional in the field

Earnings can vary based on factors such as experience, education, location, and job role.

According to data from the Bureau of Labor Statistics, the median annual wage for substance abuse, behavioral disorder, and mental health counselors was $46,240 in May 2020. However, wages can range from less than $31,750 for the bottom 10 percent to more than $78,580 for the top 10 percent.

Earnings for marriage and family therapists may vary based on their job role and location. According to the Bureau of Labor Statistics, the median annual wage for marriage and family therapists was $50,090 in May 2020. However, wages can range from less than $35,830 for the bottom 10 percent to more than $80,480 for the top 10 percent.

Overall, potential earnings for a professional in the field of mental health counseling or marriage counseling in the future will depend on a variety of factors and can vary widely. It's important to consider these factors and do your own research when considering earning potential in these fields.

Some successful figures in the niche

One of the most successful people in the field of mental health counseling is Brene Brown, a research professor, author, and speaker.

Brene is known for her research on topics such as vulnerability, shame, and empathy, and has written several best-selling books on these topics, including "Daring Greatly" and "The Gifts of Imperfection." She has also given popular TED talks on vulnerability and shame, which have been viewed millions of times.

In addition to her research and writing, Brene is also a sought-after speaker and has given presentations and workshops on topics such as leadership, creativity, and resilience.

Brene's work has been recognized with numerous awards and accolades, including the Heinz Award for her contributions to psychology and the public understanding of human emotions.

It's difficult to estimate Brene's income specifically, as she has multiple sources of income, including book sales, speaking engagements, and online courses. However, she is widely considered to be a highly successful and influential figure in the field of mental health counseling.

CHAPTER 5
AUTOMOBILE CHARGING STATION

An automobile charging station is a facility where electric vehicles (EVs) can be charged. These stations typically have one or more charging outlets and may be located in public or private locations.

There are several types of automobile charging stations, including:

Level 1 charging stations: These stations use a standard household outlet to provide a slow charge to an electric vehicle. Level 1 charging stations are typically used for overnight charging at home.

Level 2 charging stations: These stations use a higher-voltage outlet and can provide a faster charge to an electric vehicle. Level 2 charging stations are commonly found at public locations, such as shopping centers and parking garages.

Level 3 charging stations: Also known as DC fast chargers, Level 3 charging stations can provide a very fast charge to an electric vehicle. These stations are typically found at highway rest stops and other locations where long-distance travel is common.

Here are a few examples of automobile charging station businesses:

Private charging stations: Some businesses, such as hotels, restaurants, and retail stores, may install private charging stations for their customers or employees.

Public charging networks: Many cities and towns have installed public charging networks, which may include Level 2 and Level 3 charging stations. These networks may be operated by the government or by private companies.

Charging station equipment manufacturers: Companies that manufacture charging station equipment, such as charging outlets and power management systems, can also be considered as business that operate within automobile charging station industry.

Overall, automobile charging station businesses can take many forms, including private charging stations, public charging networks, and charging station equipment manufacturers.

A brief on why automobile charging station business is a business of the future.

There are several reasons why automobile charging station businesses are a business of the future:

Increased adoption of electric vehicles: As the adoption of electric vehicles (EVs) increases, the demand for charging stations is also expected to increase. According to a report by the International Energy Agency, the number of electric vehicles on the road is expected to reach 250 million by 2030. These increased demands for EVs will likely drive demand for charging stations as well.

Government incentives: Many governments around the world are encouraging the adoption of electric vehicles and have implemented incentives to support the development of charging infrastructure. For example, the US Federal government offers tax credits for the installation of charging stations, and many states have also implemented their own incentives. These incentives can make it financially attractive to start an automobile charging station business.

Environmental concerns: As concerns about climate change and air pollution increase, there is a growing push for the adoption of clean transportation technologies, such as electric vehicles. This shift towards clean transportation can create opportunities for businesses that support the adoption of EVs, including automobile charging station businesses.

Changes in consumer behavior: As the adoption of electric vehicles increases, consumer behavior is also likely to shift. For example, consumers may be more likely to choose electric vehicles for their next car purchase and may be more inclined to patronize businesses that support electric transportation, such as those that offer charging stations.

Overall, the increasing adoption of electric vehicles, government incentives, environmental concerns, and changes in consumer behavior are all factors that make automobile charging station businesses a business of the future.

How people can prepare for this?

Here are a few ways that people can prepare for a career in the automobile charging station business:

Research the market: It's important to research the market and understand the demand for charging stations in your area. Consider factors such as the number of electric vehicles in the area, the availability of charging stations, and the types of charging stations that are in demand.

Understand the technology: Familiarize yourself with the different types of charging stations and how they work. This can include learning about charging speeds, power requirements, and safety considerations.

Obtain financing: Starting an automobile charging station business can be expensive, as it may require the purchase of charging station equipment and the installation of electrical infrastructure. Consider obtaining financing to help cover these costs.

Find a suitable location: Consider factors such as accessibility, foot traffic, and visibility when selecting a location for your charging station. You may also want to consider partnering with a business or organization to host your charging station.

Build partnerships: Building partnerships with electric vehicle manufacturers, charging network providers, and other businesses can help to increase the visibility and accessibility of your charging station.

By researching the market, understanding the technology, obtaining financing, finding a suitable location, and building partnerships, you can prepare for a career in the automobile charging station business and set yourself up for success.

Five top programs that can help you be an expert in that field

Here are five programs that can help you become an expert in the field of automobile charging station businesses:

Business degree program: A business degree program, such as a Bachelor of Business Administration (BBA) or Master of Business Administration (MBA), can provide a strong foundation in business principles and practices. Coursework may include topics such as entrepreneurship, marketing, and finance, which can be helpful when starting an automobile charging station business.

Certificate program in electric vehicle charging infrastructure: Certificate programs in electric vehicle charging infrastructure can provide specialized training in the principles and practices of designing, installing, and operating charging stations. These programs may cover topics such as charging technologies, electrical infrastructure, and business management.

Online courses in electric vehicle charging infrastructure: Online courses in electric vehicle charging infrastructure can provide a comprehensive overview of the principles and practices of this field. These courses may cover topics such as charging technologies, electrical infrastructure, and business management.

Internship or apprenticeship: An internship or apprenticeship with an automobile charging station business or electric vehicle manufacturer can provide practical experience and allow individuals to learn from experienced professionals. These programs often provide hands-on training and the opportunity to work on real-world projects.

Professional certification: Professional certifications, such as the Certified Charging Station Operator (CCSO) or the Certified Electric Vehicle Supply Equipment (EVSE) Installer, can demonstrate expertise and professionalism in the field of automobile charging station businesses. These certifications may require certain levels of education and experience, as well as passing an exam.

Overall, there are many different programs and resources available for those looking to become experts in the field of automobile charging station businesses. The best option will depend on an individual's goals, interests, and schedule.

Advice for up and coming young people

Here are a few pieces of advice for upcoming young people looking to succeed in the field of automobile charging station businesses:

Believe in your ability to make a difference: Automobile charging station businesses can be rewarding and fulfilling, as you have the opportunity to contribute to the adoption of clean transportation technologies and help reduce reliance on fossil fuels. Believe in your ability to make a positive impact and let that belief motivate you to excel in your career.

Learn about the technology: Familiarize yourself with the different types of charging stations, charging technologies, and electrical infrastructure. This knowledge can help you make informed decisions when designing and operating charging stations.

Build a strong network: Building a strong network of contacts and partnerships can be key to success in the automobile charging station business. Consider joining professional organizations, attending industry events, and networking with other professionals to build relationships and share knowledge.

Stay up-to-date with industry trends: The field of electric vehicle charging infrastructure is constantly evolving, so it's important to stay up-to-date with the latest trends and best practices. Consider joining professional organizations, attending conferences, and reading industry news to stay informed about developments in the field.

Seek out mentors: Having a mentor can be a valuable resource for guidance and support. Consider seeking out mentors who are experienced professionals in the field and can provide guidance and support as you develop your career.

By learning about the technology, building a strong network, staying up-to-date with industry trends, and seeking out mentors, you can develop a positive attitude and set yourself up for success in the field of automobile charging station businesses.

Potential earnings as a professional in the field

Earnings can vary based on factors such as location, the size and scale of the business, and the number of charging stations operated.

According to data from the Bureau of Labor Statistics, the median annual wage for electric vehicle charging station installers and technicians was $49,260 in May 2020. However, wages can range from less than $31,500 for the bottom 10 percent to more than $78,200 for the top 10 percent.

Earnings for a business in the field of automobile charging station businesses can also vary widely. Factors that can impact earnings for a business include the number of charging stations operated, the location of the charging stations, and the fees charged for charging services.

Overall, potential earnings for a professional or a business in the field of automobile charging station businesses in the future will depend on a variety of factors and can vary widely. It's important to consider these factors and do your own research when considering earning potential in this field.

Some successful figures in the niche

One of the most successful people in the field of automobile charging station businesses is Elon Musk, the CEO of Tesla, Inc.

Tesla, Inc. is a leading manufacturer of electric vehicles and energy storage systems, and the company has also installed a network of charging stations around the world. Tesla's Supercharger network includes more than 20,000 charging outlets at over 3,600 locations worldwide, making it one of the largest networks of electric vehicle charging stations in the world.

In addition to his work with Tesla, Elon Musk is also known for his work in other industries, including space exploration, solar energy, and tunnel construction. He has received numerous awards and accolades for his work, including being named one of Time magazine's "100 Most Influential People" multiple times.

It's difficult to estimate Elon Musk's income specifically, as he has multiple sources of income and is the CEO of a publicly traded company. According to Forbes, Elon Musk's net worth was estimated to be $23.5 billion in 2021.

CHAPTER 6
OUTLETS FOR FAST FOOD AND DELIVERY

Fast food outlets are restaurants that specialize in serving food that is quick to prepare and serve. These establishments generally offer a limited menu of items that are prepared in advance and kept hot until they are ordered. Some fast food outlets also offer delivery services, which allow customers to have their food delivered to their home or office.

Examples of fast food outlets include McDonald's, KFC, and Burger King. These restaurants typically serve burgers, fried chicken, sandwiches, and other items that can be prepared quickly and easily. Many fast food outlets also offer sides, such as fries, onion rings, and salads, as well as drinks and desserts. Some fast food outlets also offer breakfast items, such as eggs, bacon, and sausage.

Delivery services offered by fast food outlets typically use a fleet of vehicles to transport the food to the customer's location. Customers can place orders by phone or online, and the food is typically delivered within a few hours. Some delivery services also offer the option for customers to track their order in real-time, so they know exactly when to expect their food.

A brief on why business of outlets for fast food and delivery is a business of the future.

The business of fast food outlets and delivery services is likely to continue to be successful in the future for several reasons.

First, the fast food industry has proven to be highly resilient and has continued to grow even during times of economic downturn. Fast food is often seen as a relatively inexpensive option for meals, which makes it a popular choice for consumers looking to save money.

Second, the convenience factor of fast food and delivery services is also likely to drive continued growth in the industry. With busy schedules and hectic lifestyles, many people do not have the time or inclination to cook meals at home. Fast food outlets and delivery services offer an easy and convenient way for people to get the food they want without the hassle of cooking.

Finally, advances in technology are also likely to contribute to the success of the fast food and delivery industry in the future. Online ordering and delivery apps have made it easier than ever for customers to place orders and track the status of their food, and this trend is likely to continue. In addition, the use of robots and automation in the food preparation process is also likely to increase, which could further improve efficiency and reduce costs for fast food outlets and delivery services.

How can people prepare for this?

There are several steps that people can take to prepare for a business opportunity in the fast food and delivery industry:

Research the market: It is important to thoroughly research the local market to determine the demand for fast food and delivery services, as well as the competition. This will help identify any potential gaps in the market that could be exploited.

Develop a business plan: A well-written business plan is crucial for any new business, and this is especially true for fast food and delivery ventures. The plan should outline the target market, the products or services to be offered, the marketing strategy, and the financial projections.

Secure financing: Starting a fast food or delivery business can be expensive, so it is important to secure the necessary financing in advance. This may involve seeking out loans or investors, or even crowdfunding.

Choose a location: Carefully selecting the location of the business is crucial. It should be easily accessible and visible to potential customers, with plenty of parking and good foot traffic.

Hire a team: Building a strong and reliable team is key to the success of any business. It is important to hire employees who are enthusiastic and reliable, and who have the necessary skills and experience.

Develop a strong marketing strategy: A strong marketing strategy is essential to attract and retain customers. This may involve social media advertising, email marketing, and other forms of digital marketing, as well as traditional forms of advertising such as signage and print ads.

Stay up to date with industry trends: It is important to stay informed about industry trends and developments to ensure that the business remains competitive. This may involve attending trade shows and conferences, or subscribing to industry publications.

By following these steps, individuals can position themselves to take advantage of business opportunities in the fast food and delivery industry and increase their chances of success.

Five top programs that can help you be an expert in that field

Here are five programs that can help individuals become experts in the fast food and delivery industry:

Restaurant management courses: These courses, which can be found at community colleges, universities, and online schools, provide students with a solid foundation in the principles of restaurant management. They may cover topics such as menu planning, food safety, customer service, and financial management.

Fast food industry certification programs: These programs, offered by organizations such as the National Restaurant Association, provide in-depth training on the specific practices and procedures used in the fast food industry. They may cover topics such as food safety, customer service, and menu development.

Food handling and safety courses: These courses, which may be required by state or local regulations, teach individuals how to handle food safely to prevent the spread of illness. They may cover topics such as proper food storage, cooking temperatures, and handwashing.

Marketing and advertising courses: These courses, which can be found at colleges and universities or online, teach students how to develop and implement effective marketing and advertising campaigns. They may cover topics such as market research, branding, and social media marketing.

Entrepreneurship programs: These programs, which can be found at colleges and universities or online, teach students the skills and knowledge needed to start and run their own business. They may cover topics such as business planning, financial management, and marketing.

By participating in these programs, individuals can gain the knowledge and skills needed to succeed in the fast food and delivery industry.

Advice for up and coming young people

Here are some positive attitudes and advice for upcoming young people who are looking to succeed in the fast food and delivery industry:

Be proactive: Don't wait for opportunities to come to you - create your own opportunities. Be proactive in seeking out new experiences and learning new skills that will help you succeed in the industry.

Stay positive: Keep a positive attitude, even when faced with challenges. A positive attitude can help you stay motivated and focused on your goals.

Stay organized: Good organizational skills are essential for success in any field, and the fast food and delivery industry is no exception. Stay organized and keep track of your tasks and responsibilities to ensure that you are efficient and effective in your work.

Be a team player: The fast food and delivery industry relies on teamwork, so it is important to be a good team player. Collaborate with your colleagues and support each other to achieve common goals.

Be open to learning: The fast food and delivery industry is constantly changing, so it is important to be open to learning new things. Take advantage of opportunities to learn new skills and stay up to date on industry trends.

Take care of yourself: It is important to take care of yourself, both physically and mentally, to ensure that you are able to perform your best. Make sure to eat a healthy diet, get enough sleep, and take breaks when needed.

By adopting these positive attitudes and following this advice, young people can position themselves for success in the fast food and delivery industry.

Potential earnings as a professional in the field

Earnings in as a professional or business in this sector will depend on a variety of factors such as location, demand for the business's products or services, and the individual's or business's level of experience and expertise. However, here are some general estimates of potential earnings:

For a professional:

Entry-level positions in the fast food industry, such as food prep or cashier, may pay minimum wage or slightly above. According to the Bureau of Labor Statistics, the median hourly wage for fast food workers in the United States was $11.39 in 2020.

Higher level positions, such as restaurant manager or franchise owner, may earn significantly more. The median annual wage for restaurant managers was $52,030 in 2020, according to the Bureau of Labor Statistics.

For a business:

The potential earnings for a fast food or delivery business will depend on a variety of factors such as the size of the business, the location, and the demand for the products or services offered. According to a report by IBISWorld, the fast food industry in the United States is expected to generate revenue of $246 billion in 2021, with a growth rate of 2.8% per year.

It is important to note that these estimates are provided for informational purposes only and should not be taken as definitive. Actual earnings may vary based on a number of factors.

Some successful figures in the niche

One of the most successful individuals in the fast food and delivery industry is Ray Kroc, the founder of McDonald's. Kroc was a milkshake machine salesman when he first encountered the McDonald brothers, who owned a small hamburger restaurant in California. Impressed by their efficient operation and the potential for expansion, Kroc struck a deal with the brothers to franchise their concept and expand it nationwide.

Under Kroc's leadership, McDonald's grew rapidly, and by the mid-1960s it had become a global brand with restaurants in more than 30 countries. Kroc is credited with revolutionizing the fast food industry by introducing the concept of mass production and standardization, which allowed McDonald's to consistently deliver high-quality, fast service to its customers.

In addition to its success as a restaurant chain, McDonald's has also been successful as a business, with billions of dollars in annual revenue. Today, it is one of the most recognized and successful brands in the world, with more than 38,000 restaurants in over 100 countries.

Kroc's success was due in large part to his vision and perseverance, as well as his ability to identify and capitalize on a business opportunity. His legacy lives on in the continued success of McDonald's and its impact on the fast food industry.

CHAPTER 7
INTERNET OF THINGS (IOT INDUSTRY)

The Internet of Things (IoT) refers to the growing network of physical devices, such as appliances, vehicles, and industrial equipment, that are connected to the internet and are able to collect, share, and analyze data. The IoT industry refers to the businesses and organizations that develop and offer products and services related to the IoT, such as hardware and software for connected devices, as well as the infrastructure and platforms needed to support them.

Some examples of businesses in the IoT industry include:

Hardware manufacturers: These companies design and produce the physical components of IoT devices, such as sensors, chips, and connectors.

Software developers: These companies create the software that runs on IoT devices, enabling them to collect and analyze data, as well as communicate with other devices and systems.

Infrastructure providers: These companies develop and offer the infrastructure and platforms needed to support the IoT, such as cloud computing services, data analytics platforms, and security solutions.

System integrators: These companies help businesses and organizations design and implement IoT systems, including the hardware, software, and infrastructure needed to support them.

Service providers: These companies offer services related to the IoT, such as consulting, training, and support.

By connecting billions of devices and collecting vast amounts of data, the IoT has the potential to revolutionize a wide range of industries, from healthcare and transportation to agriculture and manufacturing. The IoT industry is therefore an exciting and rapidly growing field, with many opportunities for businesses and individuals to create innovative products and services.

A brief on why Internet of Things (IoT Industry) is a business of the future.

The Internet of Things (IoT) industry is likely to continue to be a successful business in the future for several reasons:

Growing demand for connected devices: The IoT is made up of billions of connected devices, and this number is expected to continue to grow in the coming years. As more and more devices become connected, the demand for products and services related to the IoT is likely to increase.

Increasing adoption in various industries: The IoT has the potential to transform a wide range of industries, including healthcare, transportation, agriculture, and manufacturing. As more businesses and organizations adopt IoT technologies, the demand for related products and services is likely to increase.

Improved efficiency and productivity: The IoT allows businesses and organizations to collect and analyze data from connected devices in real-time, which can help improve efficiency and productivity. This is likely to make the IoT an attractive proposition for businesses looking to gain a competitive edge.

Advances in technology: As technology continues to advance, the capabilities of IoT devices are likely to improve, opening up new possibilities and applications for the technology. This could drive further growth in the IoT industry.

Overall, the IoT industry is likely to continue to be a promising business opportunity in the future, as the demand for connected devices and related products and services is expected to grow.

How can people prepare for this?

Here are some steps that individuals can take to prepare for a career or business in the Internet of Things (IoT) industry:

Gain knowledge and expertise: It is important to stay up to date on the latest trends and technologies in the IoT industry. This may involve taking courses or earning a degree in a related field, such as computer science, electrical engineering, or data analytics. It may also involve staying current with industry news and attending conferences and other events.

Build a strong network: Building a strong network of connections in the IoT industry can be beneficial for finding job opportunities and staying informed about industry developments. This may involve joining professional organizations, attending networking events, and participating in online forums and groups.

Develop a portfolio: A portfolio of relevant projects and experiences can be a valuable tool for demonstrating your skills and expertise to potential employers or clients. Consider working on side projects or internships to build up your portfolio.

Be open to new opportunities: The IoT industry is constantly evolving, so it is important to be open to new opportunities as they arise. This may involve being willing to take on new projects or roles, or even starting your own business.

Stay focused and persistent: Building a successful career or business in the IoT industry may take time and effort. It is important to stay focused on your goals and be persistent in pursuing opportunities.

By following these steps, individuals can position themselves to succeed in the IoT industry and make the most of the opportunities it offers.

Five top programs that can help you be an expert in that field

Here are five programs that can help individuals become experts in the Internet of Things (IoT) industry:

Degree programs in computer science or electrical engineering: These programs provide a strong foundation in the technical skills needed to work in the IoT industry, such as programming, computer hardware, and networking.

Data analytics programs: These programs teach students how to collect, process, and analyze data, which is an important skill in the IoT industry as connected devices generate vast amounts of data.

IoT certification programs: These programs, offered by organizations such as the IoT Academy or the Internet of Things Institute, provide in-depth training on specific aspects of the IoT, such as hardware, software, and data analytics.

Entrepreneurship programs: These programs, which can be found at colleges and universities or online, teach students the skills and knowledge needed to start and run their own business. They may cover topics such as business planning, financial management, and marketing.

Industry-specific training programs: Many companies and organizations offer training programs specifically geared towards the IoT industry. These programs can provide hands-on experience and specialized knowledge that can be valuable in the job market.

By participating in these programs, individuals can gain the knowledge and skills needed to succeed in the IoT industry.

Advice for up and coming young people

Here are some positive attitudes and advice for upcoming young people who are interested in pursuing a career or business in the Internet of Things (IoT) industry:

Be proactive: Don't wait for opportunities to come to you - create your own opportunities. Be proactive in seeking out new experiences and learning new skills that will help you succeed in the industry.

Stay positive: Keep a positive attitude, even when faced with challenges. A positive attitude can help you stay motivated and focused on your goals.

Stay organized: Good organizational skills are essential for success in any field, and the IoT industry is no exception. Stay organized and keep track of your tasks and responsibilities to ensure that you are efficient and effective in your work.

Be a team player: The IoT industry relies on teamwork, so it is important to be a good team player. Collaborate with your colleagues and support each other to achieve common goals.

Be open to learning: The IoT industry is constantly changing, so it is important to be open to learning new things. Take advantage of opportunities to learn new skills and stay up to date on industry trends.

Take care of yourself: It is important to take care of yourself, both physically and mentally, to ensure that you are able to perform your best. Make sure to eat a healthy diet, get enough sleep, and take breaks when needed.

By adopting these positive attitudes and following this advice, young people can position themselves for success in the IoT industry

Potential earnings as a professional in the field

It is difficult to predict exactly what a professional or a business in the Internet of Things (IoT) industry will earn in the future, as it will depend on a variety of factors such as location, demand for the individual's or business's products or services, and the level of experience and expertise. However, here are some general estimates of potential earnings:

For a professional:

Entry-level positions in the IoT industry, such as software developer or data analyst, may pay a starting salary of around $60,000 to $70,000 per year.

Higher level positions, such as IoT project manager or solutions architect, may earn significantly more. According to Glassdoor, the median salary for an IoT project manager in the United States is $93,106 per year, while the median salary for an IoT solutions architect is $108,076 per year.

For a business:

The potential earnings for an IoT business will depend on a variety of factors such as the size of the business, the location, and the demand for the products or services offered. According to a report by the IoT Analytics firm, the global IoT market is expected to reach $1.6 trillion in value by 2025, with a compound annual growth rate of 15.6%.

It is important to note that these estimates are provided for informational purposes only and should not be taken as definitive. Actual earnings may vary based on a number of factors.

Some successful figures in the niche

One of the most successful individuals in the Internet of Things (IoT) industry is James Park, the co-founder and CEO of Fitbit, a company that produces wearable fitness trackers and other connected devices. Park co-founded Fitbit in 2007 with the goal of helping people lead healthier lives through technology.

Under Park's leadership, Fitbit has become a leading player in the IoT industry, with a wide range of products that track everything from steps and sleep to heart rate and calories burned. The company has also forged partnerships with major healthcare providers and insurers, further expanding its reach and impact.

In addition to its success as a company, Fitbit has also been successful financially, with billions of dollars in annual revenue. The company went public in 2015 and is now listed on the New York Stock Exchange.

Park's success can be attributed to his vision and dedication to the company's mission, as well as his ability to identify and capitalize on a business opportunity in the growing IoT industry. His success has made him one of the most influential and successful figures in the IoT industry.

CHAPTER 8
BIOMETRIC SENSORS BUSINESS

A company for biometric sensors is a business that develops, produces, and sells biometric sensors, which are devices that measure and analyze biological and behavioral characteristics such as fingerprints, iris scans, and facial recognition. Biometric sensors are used in a variety of applications, including security and identification, healthcare, and consumer electronics.

Some examples of companies for biometric sensors include:

Fingerprint Cards: This Swedish company is a leading supplier of fingerprint sensors for smartphones, tablets, and other mobile devices.

Synaptics: This California-based company is a leading provider of biometric security solutions, including fingerprint scanners, facial recognition, and voice recognition.

ZK Software: This Chinese Company is a leading manufacturer of biometric security solutions, including fingerprint scanners; face recognition, and iris scanners.

EyeLock: This New York-based company is a leading provider of iris recognition technology, which is used in security, healthcare, and other applications.

Bio-Key International: This New Jersey-based company is a provider of biometric security solutions, including fingerprint scanners and voice recognition technology.

By developing and selling biometric sensors, these companies help enable secure and convenient identification and authentication in a variety of applications.

A brief on why Biometric Sensor business is a business of the future.

The business of biometric sensors is likely to continue to be a business of the future due to the increasing demand for secure and convenient identification and authentication solutions. Here are some reasons why the business for biometric sensors is expected to be successful in the future:

Growing demand for security: With the increasing amount of personal and sensitive information being stored and transmitted online, there is a growing demand for secure authentication methods. Biometric sensors, which use unique biological characteristics as a means of identification, are seen as more secure than traditional methods such as passwords, which can be easily stolen or hacked.

Convenience: Biometric sensors can provide a convenient means of identification and authentication, as they do not require the user to remember a password or carry a physical token. This makes them attractive to both consumers and businesses.

Advances in technology: As technology continues to advance, biometric sensors are becoming more accurate and reliable, as well as more affordable. This is likely to drive further adoption of biometric sensors in a variety of applications.

Increasing adoption in a variety of sectors: Biometric sensors are being adopted in a variety of sectors, including healthcare, financial services, and government. This creates opportunities for companies that develop and sell biometric sensors.

Overall, the business for biometric sensors is likely to continue to be a successful and growing field in the future due to the increasing demand for secure and convenient identification and authentication solutions.

How can people prepare for this?

Here are some steps that individuals can take to prepare for a career or business in the biometric sensor industry:

Gain knowledge and expertise: It is important to stay up to date on the latest trends and technologies in the biometric sensor industry. This may involve taking courses or earning a degree in a related field, such as electrical engineering, computer science, or biometrics. It may also involve staying current with industry news and attending conferences and other events.

Build a strong network: Building a strong network of connections in the biometric sensor industry can be beneficial for finding job opportunities and staying informed about industry developments. This may involve joining professional organizations, attending networking events, and participating in online forums and groups.

Develop a portfolio: A portfolio of relevant projects and experiences can be a valuable tool for demonstrating your skills and expertise to potential employers or clients. Consider working on side projects or internships to build up your portfolio.

Be open to new opportunities: The biometric sensor industry is constantly evolving, so it is important to be open to new opportunities as they arise. This may involve being willing to take on new projects or roles, or even starting your own business.

Stay focused and persistent: Building a successful career or business in the biometric sensor industry may take time and effort. It is important to stay focused on your goals and be persistent in pursuing opportunities.

By following these steps, individuals can position themselves to succeed in the biometric sensor industry and make the most of the opportunities it offers.

Five top programs that can help you be an expert in that field

Here are five programs that can help individuals become experts in the biometric sensor industry:

Degree programs in electrical engineering or computer science: These programs provide a strong foundation in the technical skills needed to work in the biometric sensor industry, such as circuit design, computer hardware, and software development.

Biometric certification programs: These programs, offered by organizations such as the International Association of Biometrics (IAB) or the Biometrics Institute, provide in-depth training on specific aspects of biometrics, such as fingerprint recognition, facial recognition, and iris scanning.

Data analytics programs: These programs teach students how to collect, process, and analyze data, which is an important skill in the biometric sensor industry as biometric sensors generate vast amounts of data.

Entrepreneurship programs: These programs, which can be found at colleges and universities or online, teach students the skills and knowledge needed to start and run their own business. They may cover topics such as business planning, financial management, and marketing.

Industry-specific training programs: Many companies and organizations offer training programs specifically geared towards the biometric sensor industry. These programs can provide hands-on experience and specialized knowledge that can be valuable in the job market.

By participating in these programs, individuals can gain the knowledge and skills needed to succeed in the biometric sensor industry.

Advice for up and coming young people

Here are some positive attitudes and advice for upcoming young people who are interested in pursuing a career or business in the biometric sensor industry:

Be proactive: Don't wait for opportunities to come to you - create your own opportunities. Be proactive in seeking out new experiences and learning new skills that will help you succeed in the industry.

Stay positive: Keep a positive attitude, even when faced with challenges. A positive attitude can help you stay motivated and focused on your goals.

Stay organized: Good organizational skills are essential for success in any field, and the biometric sensor industry is no exception. Stay organized and keep track of your tasks and responsibilities to ensure that you are efficient and effective in your work.

Be a team player: The biometric sensor industry relies on teamwork, so it is important to be a good team player. Collaborate with your colleagues and support each other to achieve common goals.

Be open to learning: The biometric sensor industry is constantly changing, so it is important to be open to learning new things. Take advantage of opportunities to learn new skills and stay up to date on industry trends.

Take care of yourself: It is important to take care of yourself, both physically and mentally, to ensure that you are able to perform your best. Make sure to eat a healthy diet, get enough sleep, and take breaks when needed.

By adopting these positive attitudes and following this advice, young people can position themselves for success in the biometric sensor industry.

Potential earnings as a professional in the field

Earnings will depend on a variety of factors such as location, demand for the individual's or business's products or services, and the level of experience and expertise. However, here are some general estimates of potential earnings:

For a professional:

Entry-level positions in the biometric sensor industry, such as software developer or data analyst, may pay a starting salary of around $60,000 to $70,000 per year.

Higher level positions, such as biometric sensor project manager or solutions architect, may earn significantly more. According to Glassdoor, the median salary for a biometric sensor project manager in the United States is $93,106 per year, while the median salary for a biometric sensor solutions architect is $108,076 per year.

For a business:

The potential earnings for a biometric sensor business will depend on a variety of factors such as the size of the business, the location, and the demand for the products or services offered. According to a report by the Biometrics Research Group, the global biometrics market is expected to reach $77.2 billion in value by 2022, with a compound annual growth rate of 16.9%.

It is important to note that these estimates are provided for informational purposes only and should not be taken as definitive. Actual earnings may vary based on a number of factors.

Some successful figures in the niche

One of the most successful individuals in the biometric sensor industry is Anil Jain, the Chief Executive Officer (CEO) of M2SYS Technology, a company that develops and sells biometric software and hardware solutions. Jain co-founded M2SYS in 2002 and has led the company to become a leading player in the biometric sensor industry, with products that are used in a variety of applications, including healthcare, government, and finance.

Under Jain's leadership, M2SYS has experienced significant growth, with millions of dollars in annual revenue. The company has also won numerous awards and accolades, including being named one of the fastest-growing private companies in the United States by Inc. Magazine.

In addition to his success as CEO of M2SYS, Jain is also a respected thought leader in the biometric sensor industry, with numerous publications and speaking engagements to his credit.

Jain's success can be attributed to his vision and dedication to the company's mission, as well as his ability to identify and capitalize on business opportunities in the growing biometric sensor industry. His success has made him one of the most influential and successful figures in the biometric sensor industry.

CHAPTER 9

VIRTUAL REALITY (VR)

The business of Virtual Reality (VR) refers to the development, production, and distribution of VR technology and related products and services. VR is a computer-generated simulation of a three-dimensional environment that can be interacted with in a seemingly real or physical way by a person using special equipment, such as a headset with a screen or gloves fitted with sensors. VR is used in a variety of applications, including entertainment, gaming, education, training, and healthcare.

Here are some examples of businesses in the VR industry:

Oculus: Oculus is a company that designs and manufactures VR headsets and other VR hardware. The company was founded in 2012 and was later acquired by Facebook.

HTC: HTC is a Taiwanese technology company that produces VR headsets and other VR hardware, as well as VR content and software.

Google: Google is a technology giant that has developed a number of VR products, including the Google Cardboard, a low-cost VR headset that uses a smartphone as the display, and the Google Daydream, a more advanced VR headset.

Sony: Sony is a Japanese multinational corporation that produces VR headsets and other VR hardware, as well as VR games and other content.

Unity Technologies: Unity Technologies is a software company that produces a popular game engine used for developing VR games and other VR content.

These are just a few examples of businesses in the VR industry. There are many others that develop and sell VR products and services for a variety of applications.

A brief on why Virtual Reality (VR) is a business of the future

The business of virtual reality (VR) is likely to continue to be a business of the future due to the increasing demand for immersive and interactive digital experiences. Here are some reasons why the business of VR is expected to be successful in the future:

Advancements in technology: As VR technology continues to advance; VR experiences are becoming more realistic and immersive, which is likely to drive further adoption of VR in a variety of applications.

Growing demand for entertainment: VR has the potential to revolutionize the entertainment industry by providing a more interactive and immersive experience for users. This is likely to drive demand for VR experiences in the gaming, film, and other sectors.

Increasing adoption in education and training: VR is being increasingly used as a tool for education and training, as it allows users to learn and practice skills in a simulated environment. This creates opportunities for businesses that develop VR educational content.

Business applications: VR has the potential to be used in a variety of business applications, such as product demonstrations, employee training, and virtual meetings. This creates opportunities for businesses that develop and sell VR solutions for these applications.

Overall, the business of VR is likely to continue to be a successful and growing field in the future due to the increasing demand for immersive and interactive digital experiences.

How can people prepare for this?

Here are some steps that individuals can take to prepare for a career or business in the virtual reality (VR) industry:

Gain knowledge and expertise: It is important to stay up to date on the latest trends and technologies in the VR industry. This may involve taking courses or earning a degree in a related field, such as computer science, game design, or interactive media. It may also involve staying current with industry news and attending conferences and other events.

Build a strong portfolio: A strong portfolio of VR projects and experiences can be a valuable tool for demonstrating your skills and expertise to potential employers or clients. Consider working on side projects or internships to build up your portfolio.

Network: Building a strong network of connections in the VR industry can be beneficial for finding job opportunities and staying informed about industry developments. This may involve joining professional organizations, attending networking events, and participating in online forums and groups.

Learn new skills: The VR industry is constantly evolving, so it is important to be open to learning new skills. Consider learning new software or programming languages that are relevant to the VR industry.

Be open to new opportunities: The VR industry is still in its early stages, so there are many opportunities for innovation and experimentation. Be open to new opportunities as they arise and consider starting your own business or working on new projects.

By following these steps, individuals can position themselves to succeed in the VR industry and make the most of the opportunities it offers.

Five top programs that can help you be an expert in that field

Here are five programs that can help individuals become experts in the virtual reality (VR) industry:

Degree programs in computer science or game design: These programs provide a strong foundation in the technical skills needed to work in the VR industry, such as computer programming, 3D modeling, and game design.

VR certification programs: These programs, offered by organizations such as the VR Institute of Health and Exercise or the VR/AR Association, provide in-depth training on specific aspects of VR, such as VR development, VR design, and VR health and wellness.

Data analytics programs: These programs teach students how to collect, process, and analyze data, which is an important skill in the VR industry as VR experiences generate vast amounts of data.

Entrepreneurship programs: These programs, which can be found at colleges and universities or online, teach students the skills and knowledge needed to start and run their own business. They may cover topics such as business planning, financial management, and marketing.

Industry-specific training programs: Many companies and organizations offer training programs specifically geared towards the VR industry. These programs can provide hands-on experience and specialized knowledge that can be valuable in the job market.

By participating in these programs, individuals can gain the knowledge and skills needed to succeed in the VR industry.

Advice for up and coming young people

Here are some positive attitudes and advice for upcoming young people who are interested in pursuing a career or business in the virtual reality (VR) industry:

Be proactive: Don't wait for opportunities to come to you - create your own opportunities. Be proactive in seeking out new experiences and learning new skills that will help you succeed in the industry.

Stay positive: Keep a positive attitude, even when faced with challenges. A positive attitude can help you stay motivated and focused on your goals.

Stay organized: Good organizational skills are essential for success in any field, and the VR industry is no exception. Stay organized and keep track of your tasks and responsibilities to ensure that you are efficient and effective in your work.

Be a team player: The VR industry relies on teamwork, so it is important to be a good team player. Collaborate with your colleagues and support each other to achieve common goals.

Be open to learning: The VR industry is constantly changing, so it is important to be open to learning new things. Take advantage of opportunities to learn new skills and stay up to date on industry trends.

Take care of yourself: It is important to take care of yourself, both physically and mentally, to ensure that you are able to perform your best. Make sure to eat a healthy diet, get enough sleep, and take breaks when needed.

By adopting these positive attitudes and following this advice, young people can position themselves for success in the VR industry.

Potential earnings as a professional in the field

For a professional:

Entry-level positions in the VR industry, such as VR developer or VR designer, may pay a starting salary of around $60,000 to $70,000 per year.

Higher level positions, such as VR project manager or VR solutions architect, may earn significantly more. According to Glassdoor, the median salary for a VR project manager in the United States is $86,176 per year, while the median salary for a VR solutions architect is $101,873 per year.

For a business:

The potential earnings for a VR business will depend on a variety of factors such as the size of the business, the location, and the demand for the products or services offered. According to a report by the VR/AR Association, the VR/AR market is expected to reach $215 billion in value by 2021, with a compound annual growth rate of 121.3%.

It is important to note that these estimates are provided for informational purposes only and should not be taken as definitive. Actual earnings may vary based on a number of factors.

Some successful figures in the niche

One of the most successful individuals in the virtual reality (VR) industry is John Carmack, the Chief Technology Officer (CTO) of Oculus VR, a company that develops and sells VR hardware and software products. Carmack co-founded Oculus VR in 2012 and has played a key role in the development of the company's VR products, including the Oculus Rift headset.

Under Carmack's leadership, Oculus VR has experienced significant growth and has become a leading player in the VR industry. In 2014, Facebook acquired Oculus VR for $2 billion, making it one of the most successful acquisitions in the VR industry.

In addition to his success as CTO of Oculus VR, Carmack is also a respected thought leader in the VR industry, with numerous publications and speaking engagements to his credit.

Carmack's success can be attributed to his technical expertise and his vision for the future of VR. His success has made him one of the most influential and successful figures in the VR industry.

CHAPTER 10
VETERINARIANS

Veterinarians are medical professionals who provide medical care to animals, including pets, livestock, and wildlife. They diagnose and treat animal health problems, perform surgeries, and advise owners on how to care for their animals.

The business of veterinarians involves providing medical care to animals and promoting animal health. This may involve working in a variety of settings, such as private practices, animal hospitals, zoos, or research laboratories.

Examples of veterinarians and their businesses include:

A small animal veterinarian who owns a private practice that provides medical care to pets, such as dogs, cats, and birds.

A large animal veterinarian who works on ranches or farms and provides medical care to livestock, such as cows, horses, and goats.

A zoo veterinarian who works at a zoo and provides medical care to a variety of animals, including exotic species.

A research veterinarian who works in a laboratory setting and conducts medical research on animals.

Overall, the business of veterinarians is dedicated to promoting the health and well-being of animals and helping to improve their quality of life.

A brief on why Veterinarians is a business of the future.

The business of veterinarians is likely to continue to be a business of the future due to the increasing demand for animal health care and the growing importance of animal welfare. Here are some reasons why the business of veterinarians is expected to be successful in the future:

Increasing pet ownership: The number of pets owned by households is expected to continue to increase in the future, which is likely to drive demand for veterinary services. According to the American Pet Products Association, 66% of households in the United States own a pet, and this number is expected to continue to grow.

Growing awareness of animal welfare: There is increasing awareness of the importance of animal welfare and the need for high-quality medical care for animals. This is likely to drive demand for veterinarians who are skilled in providing compassionate and high-quality care.

Advances in veterinary medicine: As veterinary medicine continues to advance, veterinarians will be able to offer more advanced and specialized medical care to animals. This is likely to increase demand for their services.

Increasing demand for alternative therapies: There is growing interest in alternative therapies for pets, such as acupuncture and herbal medicine. This creates opportunities for veterinarians who are trained in these therapies.

Overall, the business of veterinarians is likely to continue to be a successful and growing field in the future due to the increasing demand for animal health care and the growing importance of animal welfare.

How can people prepare for this?

Here are some steps that individuals can take to prepare for a career or business in the veterinary industry:

Earn a degree in veterinary medicine: In order to become a veterinarian, individuals must earn a Doctor of Veterinary Medicine (DVM) degree from an accredited veterinary school. This typically requires completing a four-year program that includes coursework in biology, chemistry, and animal anatomy, as well as clinical training.

Obtain a license: In order to practice veterinary medicine, individuals must be licensed in the state where they plan to work. Licensing requirements vary by state, but typically involve passing a licensing exam and completing a certain number of hours of clinical training.

Gain experience: Gaining experience in the veterinary field can be beneficial for building skills and knowledge, as well as for networking and finding job opportunities. Consider volunteering at a veterinary clinic or animal shelter, or completing an internship or externship.

Stay current with industry developments: It is important to stay up to date on the latest trends and developments in the veterinary industry. This may involve attending conferences, joining professional organizations, and reading industry publications.

Develop business skills: If you are interested in starting your own veterinary business, it is important to develop business skills such as financial management, marketing, and customer service. Consider taking courses or earning a degree in business or entrepreneurship.

By following these steps, individuals can position themselves for success in the veterinary industry and make the most of the opportunities it offers.

Five top programs that can help you be an expert in that field

Here are five programs that can help individuals become experts in the veterinary industry:

Doctor of Veterinary Medicine (DVM) degree program: This is the primary degree program for individuals who want to become veterinarians. DVM programs typically last four years and include coursework in biology, chemistry, and animal anatomy, as well as clinical training.

Veterinary Technician degree program: This program is designed for individuals who want to work as veterinary technicians, which are medical professionals who assist veterinarians in caring for animals. Veterinary technician programs typically last two to three years and include coursework in animal anatomy, physiology, and nursing.

Veterinary residency programs: These programs are designed for veterinarians who want to specialize in a particular area of veterinary medicine, such as surgery, internal medicine, or neurology. Residency programs typically last one to three years and involves advanced training in a specific area of veterinary medicine.

Master of Science in Veterinary Science (MSVS) degree program: This program is designed for veterinarians who want to pursue advanced training in a specific area of veterinary medicine. MSVS programs typically last one to two years and involve coursework and research in a specific area of veterinary science.

Veterinary Business Management Certificate program: This program is designed for veterinarians who want to learn business skills such as financial management, marketing, and customer service. The program typically involves coursework and may be completed online or in person.

By participating in these programs, individuals can gain the knowledge and skills needed to succeed in the veterinary industry.

Advice for up and coming young people

Here are some positive attitudes and advice for upcoming young people who are interested in pursuing a career or business in the veterinary industry:

Be passionate about animals: A strong passion for animals is essential for success in the veterinary industry. If you are not already passionate about animals, consider exploring different types of animal-related work to see if it is something that interests you.

Work hard: The veterinary industry is competitive and requires a high level of dedication and hard work. Be prepared to put in the time and effort to succeed in your studies and in your career.

Stay current with industry developments: The veterinary industry is constantly evolving, so it is important to stay up to date on the latest trends and developments. This may involve attending conferences, joining professional organizations, and reading industry publications.

Be a team player: The veterinary industry relies on teamwork, so it is important to be a good team player. Collaborate with your colleagues and support each other to achieve common goals.

Be open to learning: The veterinary industry is constantly changing, so it is important to be open to learning new things. Take advantage of opportunities to learn new skills and stay up to date on industry trends.

Take care of yourself: Working in the veterinary industry can be physically and emotionally demanding, so it is important to take care of yourself to ensure that you are able to perform your best. Make sure to eat a healthy diet, get enough sleep, and take breaks when needed.

By adopting these positive attitudes and following this advice, young people can position themselves for success in the veterinary industry.

Potential earnings as a professional in the field

For a professional:

According to the U.S. Bureau of Labor Statistics (BLS), the median annual wage for veterinarians in the United States was $95,460 in May 2021.

Veterinarians who work in private practice or who own their own business may earn more than this, depending on the success of their business and the demand for their services.

For a business:

The potential earnings for a veterinary business will depend on a variety of factors such as the size of the business, the location, and the demand for the products or services offered. According to a report by the American Veterinary Medical Association, the demand for veterinary services is expected to increase in the coming years, which may lead to increased earnings for veterinary businesses.

It is important to note that these estimates are provided for informational purposes only and should not be taken as definitive. Actual earnings may vary based on a number of factors.

Some successful figures in the niche

One of the most successful individuals in the veterinary industry is Dr. Marty Becker, a veterinarian and author who has made a significant impact in the field of animal health care. Becker is the Chief Veterinary Correspondent for ABC News and has appeared on numerous television programs, including Good Morning America and The Dr. Oz Show.

In addition to his work as a veterinarian and media personality, Becker has also authored several best-selling books on animal health care and has founded several organizations that promote animal welfare, including the Fear Free initiative, which aims to reduce fear, anxiety, and stress in pets during veterinary visits.

Becker's success can be attributed to his expertise in veterinary medicine and his ability to communicate complex medical concepts to a wide audience. His success has made him one of the most influential and successful figures in the veterinary industry.

EPILOGUE

As the world continues to evolve and technology advances at a rapid pace, it is clear that the businesses of the future will be shaped by innovation and a willingness to embrace change. The 10 businesses profiled in this book represent just a small sample of the types of companies that will thrive in the years to come. From renewable energy to virtual reality, these businesses are poised to make a significant impact on the world. They are not only creating new products and services, but also finding innovative ways to solve some of the most pressing problems of our time.

As we look ahead, it is important to remember that the future is not set in stone. The businesses of tomorrow will be shaped by the actions we take today. It will be up to entrepreneurs, policymakers, and consumers alike to pave the way for a sustainable and equitable future. Innovation will continue to drive economic growth, but it will also be important to ensure that the benefits of this growth are shared widely. The businesses of the future must strive to create value for all stakeholders, not just shareholders. They must also be mindful of their impact on the environment and society as a whole.

As this book comes to a close, we can only imagine the amazing and impactful businesses that will come in the future, and hope that they will inspire us all to be agents of positive change in the world